PROCLAIMING the PROMISE

Reflections on the God of Love

RUTH PATTERSON

VERITAS

First published 2006 by
Veritas Publications
7/8 Lower Abbey Street
Dublin 1
Ireland
Email publications@veritas.ie
Website www.veritas.ie

ISBN 1 84730 007 3 / 978 1 84730 007 2

10 9 8 7 6 5 4 3 2 1

A catalogue record for this book
is available from the British Library.

Printed in the Republic of Ireland
by Betaprint Ltd., Dublin

Veritas books are printed on paper made from the wood pulp of managed forests. For every tree felled, at least one tree is planted, thereby renewing natural resources.

Contents

To all the Friends of Restoration Ministries who have believed in the promise and are courageously living it.

Foreword

There is a very short account of a homeless woman in one of Rachel Naomi Remen's books that can serve as a marvelously heart-wrenching and mind-stopping introduction to this book. One of her colleagues, a psychiatrist like her, sees people who live on the street gratis once a month. And this one woman who lives inseparable from her shopping cart climbs one of the steepest hills in San Francisco to get to his office. But she will not leave the shopping cart anywhere – she's afraid of being robbed and of losing all her possessions. So she starts the climb up the hill and carries a rope with her, tied at one end to the shopping cart. When she gets to a parking meter, she pulls the cart up behind her. Then she climbs again, and then drags the cart behind her. It blocks up the incline and it takes hours with her needing to rest periodically. It is hard enough for her to do when she comes once a month for her hour-long session with the doctor.

But the nurses in his office say that she comes more often than that – she comes sometimes once or twice a week. She goes into the office, ignores them except for a nod and then stands on the threshold of his office, in the doorway. They repeatedly tell her that he is not in, but she doesn't seem to care – she isn't looking for him. She stands on the threshold and just looks into the room and stays there silently, sometimes for ten or fifteen minutes or a half hour and then turns around, nods to them and goes back out to her shopping cart and starts the long journey down the hill. When the nurses asked the doctor about it and what she was doing, he paused before answering. 'I think,' he said, 'that she comes back to this place and stands on the threshold because she knows that entering into that room is important. It's hard and it's emotional, filled with tears and laughter, but it's always filled with insight and understanding – what is giving her meaning – to her past and why she lives on the street and what that means – and if she could ever go back to living like other people do. She knows that I will only be there once a month to see her, but she comes and stands on the threshold to see herself and what she's like when she talks with me – she comes to see herself and to remember when she needs it. And she does her own hard work alone when she discovers something and then, she will have it in her mind when she comes to talk to me about it.'

The threshold – for most of us, a threshold is for passing over, crossing over into a room or exiting and we barely think about it. How often do we stand on a threshold in a doorway, the entrance to a house or a building, or even at a gate or a door and just stand there before we enter? Oddly enough that's what this book is all about: thresholds. Each short reflection – they alternate between prose introductions and more free verse reflections – serves as a threshold. The book begins with the thresholds of seasons of the liturgical year, Advent/Christmas, and then jumps to Lent/Easter and then ordinary time reflections that can come whenever, out of the blue, the product of long keeping and letting it sift and percolate. But you don't have to read the book liturgically – many of us find ourselves often out of synch with the liturgical year because of what is happening historically in the public arena or what is happening to us personally in our families, our work and our spiritual lives. The Spirit doesn't always follow liturgical time sequences.

A threshold – you can't read this book quickly. You do have to stop, arrested – and after the introduction piece, stand on a threshold or, if you know that you're going to be there a while, get comfortable in your favourite chair, pew in church, or a wall or place outdoors so that you can mull over and reflect at your leisure. Ruth Patterson's words sound familiar and they speak of things we all experience but they have a character that stops us in our tracks and nudges us to savour, to wonder, to question and examine, and cull from her wisdom into the vagaries of our lives.

Thresholds – Ruth has lived like the rest of us, with family and job, loss and grief, nephews and nieces, loneliness and solitude, in church and in the world. She has also lived in a specific historical period, in the north of Ireland – the last sixty years and so the thresholds also, of necessity, deal with torture, insecurity, disappearances, brutality, murder, the indignities and horrors that human beings are capable of and do to one another in the name of sectarian politics, economics/poverty and religion. Sometimes the reflections are singularly personal and yet they are always turned to shift light and focus on the universal experience of struggling to live with grace in the face of evil and the consequences of just being alive in the world at this time.

And like the woman in the story with all that she owns piled in her shopping cart that she won't part with, even when dragging them around with her, that makes her life incredibly more difficult than necessary – most of us will approach this book in the same way. Oh, we don't have a shopping cart and we're not that obvious about what we carry around with us, but we're just as attached to so much in the past that impacts our present realities – burdens we have been given by others, memories, things we have done and not dealt with, huge questions that don't have answers, or they seem to get answered and then they spring up and bow us down yet again. Each of us needs a place, a friend, a time and words to help us return to ourselves, to see ourselves and how we do fit into the rest of the world, others' lives and into the kingdom of God and the will of God.

God – God is laced through all of these pieces. There is the God of the Scriptures, the Word of God made flesh in Jesus, incarnated human, as one of us. There is the God of Jesus, the beloved Father who is Jesus' constant companion whom he seeks to delight and reveal with his words and his presence, to all in the world he dwells in, and those he dwells among. And there is the God of the Spirit that is given in gifts for others and in insight and power – to survive the twists and unexpected drops and dark holes that are a part of life often because of the actions of other people, along with the shared joy and everyday pleasures. There is the God that is the sacrament of the world and a dialogue with this God, seeking to understand the languages of history, of political issues, of violence and death that is stupid and unnecessary and only contributes to despair and making life so much more of a burden than a delight. And there is the God of the Trinity, of community, of family that seeks to draw everyone into its embrace. This is the God that Ruth Patterson has met, often enough to come to know a little, and this is the God that seeps out in these pages.

Life and the world of the last sixty years have been different than much of time that has transpired and gone before 1945. There has been the atom bomb, the end of the Second World War with the calculated terror of Nagasaki and Hiroshima. There have been more wars since: the Vietnam war, the cold war, the arms race war and countless internecine wars that people must deal with close to home – in the Middle East, in Latin America and Southeast Asia, and, for Ruth Patterson, the war of hate, of crime and terrorist attacks of Northern Ireland – called the 'Troubles' euphemistically. This closeness and nearness, this ordinary everyday threat of evil impacts and shadows every moment and every relationship, including our inner life of prayer, penance and the struggle to be just and truthful and reconciling. And these public issues Ruth Patterson has struggled with – not to be overcome by them or embittered, but to redeem them, to draw forth hope from them and see them in the shadow of the cross and resurrection of Jesus. And it is in this regard that these reflections perhaps can touch us most deeply, scratch at our comfortableness and accommodations and prod us to bring the Gospel, the Good News of God in Jesus to bear on what is happening in our world, in our history, now.

Ruth works at Restoration Ministries in Belfast, a small group that seeks to draw people together in conversation and to honestly look at differences, especially in regards to religion and politics – often of long-standing intense emotional feelings and prejudices, as well as experiences. We bring so much hurt, so much repressed anger and fear, so much unresolved hate and human loss to our daily lives and encounters. And these are so often exacerbated by events and public personages who play on these personal weaknesses and human failings to escalate violence and deepen these gulfs between us. It is painfully hard to just get in touch with one another and to stay in touch with anyone who is not of our immediate circle of trusted kin and friends. This is what the work of Restoration Ministries is about – not just for those in the city of Belfast, or in Northern Ireland, but also for the country at large.

There is a remarkable medieval story that gives one a sense of the emotional impact and the theological ponderings of this book. I'll tell you the name I give it at the end of the story. Once upon a time a young woman was expelled from heaven because even though she had lived a not unusual life, she still harboured a lot of resentment and lack of compassion for others – and there were many she hoped would not make it into heaven because of things they had done to hurt her and those she loved. As she was leaving heaven, one of the others watching her go leaned over and whispered that they'd let her back in if she could bring back a gift for God – one of the few things that God valued more than so many other gifts that were often given. And so she travelled the earth looking for gifts – things she thought that God might take delight in and so let her come in to stay.

She made so many trips back and forth to heaven bearing the gifts carefully chosen and acquired from earth. There were things like a faded photograph of a couple who had been faithful for so many years; the last coins that an old man had given to someone even poorer than himself; there was a child's toy given to another though the toy was her favourite. There was the blood of a martyr shed in witness to the faith and the washcloth of a woman who had cared for her elderly parents for a decade, along with a missionary's cross that was the only possession they had from their home country. But she wasn't let back in.

One day she was sitting in a small village, at a fountain, just watching and wondering if she'd ever be let back into heaven – she felt like crying but that wouldn't help – she had to find another gift. As she sat there forlorn and alone she noticed some young children playing and that they were slowly inching their way closer to the fountain and all of a sudden they were up and over the edge and into the water! They were splashing each other, dripping wet and laughing with wild glee. A man rode up just at that moment. He was wearied with battle and killing and thirsty and just wanting to get home from war. He got down from his horse and bent to drink from the fountain and noticed the children so filled with joy and his heart lurched. He remembered his own childhood and how filled with hope he had been, so filled with dreams and possibility and he saw his own reflection in the water and wept. He wept for shame, for loss, for repentance, for forgiveness, knowing all he had done; the harm he had inflicted on others and what he had lost of his own integrity. He wondered if his soul looked as torn and shredded as his clothing and as soiled and bloodied as his armour – and he wept and wept. She moved quickly and silently, unseen and caught one of his tears and turned for heaven. She found herself on the threshold of heaven and realised that she herself was weeping in gratitude for mercy and for joy. I call it 'The Tear'.

On every page of this book are tears – of gratitude, of loss and pain, of fear from the long shadows of terror that are always vague, and sometimes specific in their evil and of joy from the simple pleasures of the birth of a child, a marriage, a dinner shared with friends and moments of adoration, of the beauty of the earth and the lingering absence that is often the experience of our God. It is a very Irish book, as my Nana would say – meaning that 'life is a glorious thing, if you don't weaken – and if you do, then when you stagger and fall, get up and make a piece of poetry out of it, sing for God's sake and grasp hold of someone and hold on for a dearer life'.

And there are tears that are shared around the world. In one of my visits to Ireland in the last years, to the west coast, the three of us travelling together stopped at a Chinese restaurant in Galway. It was a most amazing universal experience. One of my companions had spent years in China, the other in South America as missionaries and we had conversations in Mandarin with the owner, in Spanish with the busboy and the girl who brought our food taught us words in Gaelic, while the couple visiting at the table next to us was from Bosnia, and we spoke with them in English, and smatterings of Italian and Arabic. This book in its own small way is a place of refuge, of sanctuary gleaned from a life of truly living and a threshold – an invitation to enter and know the presence of heaven, that is as much here on earth as anywhere else. Catherine of Siena proclaimed in hope that 'For anyone who believes in Jesus the Crucified risen from the dead, then all the way home to heaven, is heaven!' This book will steadfastly remind us of that reality, in the midst of a world veiled in tears and laughter. Turn the pages and begin the habit of standing hesitant, expectant and consciously on thresholds.

Megan McKenna
Albuquerque, New Mexico
September 2006

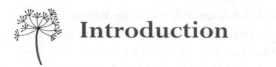 # Introduction

Words have always fascinated me. It is not so much the words themselves, but the wealth, the depth and often the subtlety of meaning behind them. Some people use too many words; some use too few. Over the last years in Northern Ireland so many words have been used, often in a condemnatory or a preachy sense, that they have lost something of their potency and their effectiveness. People are weary of yet more words without any action. Perhaps what we need more than anything else is the space, the safety and the peace to hear for ourselves the Word embodied in the person and the Spirit of Jesus. So why am I writing a book and presenting the reader with yet more words? I think it is simply because when I have taken the space and allowed myself to be embraced, even for a short while, by peace, these reflections have been given and the only way they can be expressed is through words. They are not definitive statements on anything, but if they lead you, the reader, to some sort of encounter with the Word, and if in that encounter you catch some glimpse of the unseen world that is all about us, or feel yourself embraced, however fleetingly, by peace or love or hope, then perhaps this little book can be some sort of travelling companion through the busy and the sometimes lonely world that is our life.

This book is a collection of reflections written at different times: many of them for the monthly newsletter of Restoration Ministries where I work; others were written for very specific occasions, some because I might have been very moved by a particular happening, some because my spirit seems to be more alert or sensitised at particular times during the Christian Year, such as Advent or Easter. It is as if I am picking up the rhythm of the Spirit behind the words. I hope that, in some small way, as you read these reflections that may be your experience too.

I would like to thank Ruth Garvey and the team in Veritas for their work in bringing this collection of reflections together.

Advent

Advent is a very special time in the Christian year. For me, it is as if I am standing on tiptoe in my spirit, waiting for something to happen. It is a threshold time where I am standing on the brink of something mighty about to break in from the unseen, but very real world. Advent is a season when past, present and future come together, where eternity breaks into time, so that, in any one moment, I can be present with the shepherds outside Bethlehem, listening in wonder to the angels' song and the amazing message they brought; I can be very aware right now that Jesus is here and very near; and I can be caught up in very fleeting glimpses of the Kingdom that is all about us, but is, paradoxically, still to come.

A new day is dawning for us in Northern Ireland after so many years of civil unrest and political instability, although that day often seems to be slow in coming. On a wider scale global insecurity and faltering confidence are the hallmarks of this present era. Dark clouds of apprehension and fear, made more menacing by the sense of impermanence of all that we hold dear, threaten to force us to retreat to the womb of our own particular tribe or culture, race or religion. In the midst of so much chaos and weariness how can we begin again? The season of Advent reminds us that in spite of all that is shadowy and dark in our community and in the world at large we are in the season of hope, the season of restoration. We are called, all of us, not to strive to hold back the dark, and sometimes it can be very, very dark, but rather to enter into the heart of it with the confidence of an Advent people whose hallmarks are hope, joy, peace, faith and love.

At the moment we are in an in-between time. An in-between time can seem a bit like a wilderness, a place where we can easily lose our way. The destination can become uncertain and the temptation is to sit down and passively wait for things to be different and to lose all sense of journeying or of beginning again. In human terms we could possibly be justified in thinking and feeling like this. But actually, this in-between time is perhaps the most challenging and the most exciting of all, for those with eyes to see. It is a time when we passionately wait for God to break in, for the new thing that he is doing. It is a time when we trust enough to keep journeying, even when we do not see the way ahead too clearly. It is a time when we affirm the promises of God that the wilderness period we have known is going to rejoice, that the desert places in our community life and in our world are going to blossom like the rose.

 **Advent**

I wonder
will God begin again
with us
this
Christmas?

Two thousand years
since he began before
in such a little,
mighty way,
two thousand years
since heaven stood
on tiptoe
and all creation
held its breath,
as one little,
faithful soul
said 'yes'
and opened up the way
for God to come;
two thousand years ago
God spoke,
and into the darkness,
into the night,
into the shadows
of our exiled state
he came
in Jesus.
God saw that it was good

and Light
began to shine.

There was another time,
so long ago,
before the dawn of history,
when God
who was and is
and evermore shall be,
looked out on emptiness,
on formless masses
cloaked in darkness,
and decided to begin.
He spoke.
He saw that it was good
and Light
began to shine.

But Darkness
armed itself for war,
willing once again
the chaos
where it would be
at home,
and, wanting to usurp
the place of God,
used the flower
of all of God's creation,
the beloved of his heart,

to seek
to overcome
the Light.

Some, not all
were true,
courageous bearers
of the flickering flame,
prophetic voices
for the tender
aching heart
of One
who never ceased
to look with love
on all that
he had made,
and even
in the midst
of darkness
to see that
it was good.

So, when the time
was right,
two thousand years ago
God dealt
a shattering blow
to Darkness.
He spoke His Word,
and Living Flame,
Unconquerable Light
began to shine.

Two thousand years,
and we,

the present bearers
of that living Flame,
cry out for God
to once again
begin.

For Darkness stalks the earth
so powerfully still.
Yet, in the midst
of seeming victory,
we know its doom
is once for all foretold.
The Flame still burns.
The Light still shines.
And now the time is ours.

Does God still look
on all that
he has made
and see that it is good?
Is there within the heart
of God
the hope
and the desire
to once again
begin?

Perhaps my prayer
should be
'Begin again,
O God
in me'.

If I,
a little, stumbling,
faithful soul
say 'yes',
and others
in so many other places
do the same,
then once again,
all heaven
will stand on tiptoe,
and all creation
hold its breath,
as in our day
the way is opened up
for God to come.

I wonder,
will God begin again
with us
this Christmas?

The Herald

John the Baptist is an Advent figure. He is the great, prophetic preparer, fully focused on his vocation to get people into the right state of readiness for the coming of Jesus. There were many women and men involved in the outworking of God's master plan of salvation, each one of them playing their part; the prophets of old who foretold his coming, Elizabeth and Zechariah, Mary and Joseph, Simeon and Anna, and then John, perhaps the greatest of all the prophets, described by Isaiah centuries before as 'a voice shouting in the wilderness'. He challenged people to take a good look at their lives, their attitudes, their ways of behaving, to turn from their sins and to turn towards God. They were to prepare a road for the Lord's coming. In ancient times there was no roads' service. There were worn paths or roadways of sorts, and tracks or trails. But whenever a king was coming to visit a particular town or city, then the residents of that place had to prepare the roads for his coming. They had to fill in the hollows and level the humps, and altogether make as smooth and as straight a road as possible. Just as in the natural so in the realm of the soul, John knew that there were many rough places to be made smooth and many twisted bits to be straightened out. He basically told people that they needed to repent, to begin to see things differently, to get their act together if they wanted to be ready for the coming of the Messiah. He was fearless in his proclamation because he knew what he hoped for and he believed that the promises of God would be fulfilled. To be such a preparer of the way cost him dearly: in the end it cost him his life. He was a man of destiny and he fulfilled that destiny. There is a time for everything, a season for every purpose under heaven. He knew the right time for him and he seized it, to the glory of God. This was his moment to play his part in the coming of the Kingdom that was to be fully embodied in the person of Jesus.

John recognised his moment and grabbed it. If we pick up the mantle of the preparers, we are making an investment for the future. We are preparing the way for something bigger to happen. It doesn't matter if we're not in at the finish (John wasn't), because the finish is God's business. So long as we level a few mountains and hills, and fill in a few valleys, we contribute to and are in the process of fulfilling our destiny. Now is the only time we've got. This is our time and it is in this time that our Advent God calls us to be on tiptoe in preparation for what is yet to come. Today is preparation time for the future, for tomorrow, but this moment is also sacred and special and, paradoxically, stands on its own. God is here right now, Emmanuel, God with us, and yet to come. That's the mystery that the anointed preparers live with and in. It gives them the courage to shout out, to be heralds of good news that may well upset the status quo and so cost them dear.

The Herald

A voice cries out in the wilderness,
'Prepare the way for the Lord'.
And people flock there to find him,
this prophet who utters a word
unambivalent in its condemning
of power seeking, lying and greed,
yet offering hope to the penitent
who will turn to God in their need.

A voice cries out in the wilderness,
'Raise the valleys, make rough places plain,
level mountains and straighten what's crooked.
Remove any tarnish or stain.
Let all that is wrong now be righted,
let your lives show you've started anew,
for the One who was promised is coming
to sift out the false from the true.

He is coming, my Lord and my Saviour,
he is coming, my Master, my King.
And I, John, am only the herald.
It's God's word and God's timing I bring.'
But that voice crying out in the desert
shocked the powers that be to their core.
In their fear and their anger they took him,
and the wilderness heard him no more.

Yet his voice echoes down through the ages,
and his message is relevant still,
'Turn to God from self-centred living,

seek justice and peace and good will
for all those oppressed and downtrodden,
imprisoned in anguish and pain
who feel that the world has forgotten
and who look for God's coming in vain.'

Where are those who will pick up John's mantle
and seek to be prophets today?
So often their voices are silenced.
There's no one to point out the way.
Corruption, greed, fear are our masters
in this wilderness, what can we do?
Pray for voices to speak out with courage,
and someday that voice could be you.

For the crust of the earth is moving,
and that which was rooted now shakes,
and the air around us is thundering,
as the whole of the universe quakes.
Our world is on tiptoe for Advent,
though most of us don't have a clue
that the One who was promised is coming
to sift out the false from the true.

Let our voices ring out with conviction,
let our lives become icons of love,
of justice and truth and compassion,
and the wisdom that comes from above.
In all of earth's wilderness anguish,
in its sinning, its loss and its pain,
let a road once more open for us,
as we welcome his coming again.

The Angels' Song

Preparation begins to release in us a joy as we realise that that for which we have been hoping and preparing for so long is getting nearer. I know that time is not a factor in heaven and it is hard for us who are grounded in time and space to conceive of that which is far more. In the end, it is mystery. But if I can use our language for now, did you ever wonder how long God had been preparing for this particular moment when he would break into time, into history in this remarkable, unthinkable way with his amazing, loving plan of salvation for all humankind? I find that thought absolutely amazing. It is a love that goes beyond any words to describe that God, knowing from the beginning what way he would have to take, in the person of Jesus, still went ahead with his loving purposes in creation. And when the time was right, God acted. Everything was in place. I wonder were the angels aware of his preparations? When he spoke the words, 'This is it. It's action time', I am sure that the heavenly hosts could hardly contain themselves with joy! That joy burst onto an earthly scenario in the night sky over Bethlehem. First of all their leader appeared to an audience chosen by God, some of the humblest and poorest of the land: 'Don't be afraid. I bring you good news of great joy for everyone. The Saviour – yes, the Messiah, the Lord – has been born tonight in Bethlehem the city of David.' And then, all of a sudden, he was joined by a vast host of others – the armies of heaven – this time not out to do battle with the warring hosts of Satan, but to add their voices to the greatest celebration of joy and the greatest announcement of all time: 'Glory to God in the highest heaven, and peace on earth to all whom God favours.' They were heralds, those who prepared the way, forerunners, with important news to announce. Heralds were vital in the ancient world. They were the chief means of communicating that something was about to happen. In this instance, the news was mind-blowing! God was coming to earth and the herald angels were sent with a message to prepare people's hearts to receive the new-born King. In the tired, broken, hard world to which they came with their song, only a few heard it, a few of the poor, the little, the rejected, but they were enough. This one moment of sheer, unadulterated joy would have more than compensated for the weary, poverty-stricken drudgery of their lives. They had heard the angels' song and they had seen with their own eyes the fulfilment of God's promise.

The Angels' Song

I stand on the threshold
of Advent,
my whole being on tiptoe,
waiting and listening
and scanning the horizons
of my soul
to hear an angel singing.

This weary, warring world
unwittingly
stands also on a threshold,
but not on tiptoe, not
waiting,
or listening in expectancy
for a song to pierce
its night with stars of hope.
Overwhelmed by busyness
and threat of war,
by famine and disease,
by floods and fires,
it waits, instead,
to see
the angel of death appear
in all of its avenging power.

Yet, in the midst
of seeming total blackness,
for those with ears to hear
and hearts to understand,
faintly and from far away

a song begins
to soar.
At first its tune
is not familiar,
its words not understood,
but as these faithful souls,
drawn from every tribe
and race and nation
take time to stop and listen,
the lyrics come
with unmistakable truth
and hope and beauty,
'Glory to God
in highest heaven
and peace on earth
to those on whom
his favour rests'.

The armies of heaven's
angels
proclaim the promise
and the gift of God,
and, as I stand
on the threshold of Advent,
I believe,
and what is more, I know,
I hear the angels singing.

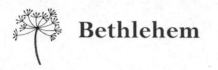 # Bethlehem

Perhaps the most significant journey we will ever make is the one to Bethlehem where we each discover in our own time and in our own way God born for us, God present for us, for each of us individually and for all of us together. It is a road we may have to travel not once but many times as we are drawn into a deeper understanding of what it means to be a friend of Jesus in this confusing, frightening, weary and often despairing world in which we live. Yet it is also a world filled with opportunity and promise. This is the world that our children and our grandchildren are going to inherit. How will they live it with confidence, awareness and compassion? The answer, it seems to me, lies in travelling the road to 'Bethlehem', the little road that is the way of openness, of trust, of faithfulness, of obedience and of love.

Bethlehem

Bethlehem,
I hear the name
and for an instant
it evokes
memories of
childhood,
of Christmas
expectation,
of wonders in the
night,
of stars and
shepherds,
of kings and angels,
of eternity bursting
into time,
of heaven rejoicing,
and God
so very near.

Bethlehem,
I hear the name
on television news,
place of pilgrimage
become a
battleground,
symbol of hatred
and division,
Royal David's city
raped and

wounded,
bullet-ridden, no
wonders in the
night,
no stars, no angels,
and God
so far away.

Bethlehem
then and now.
How can we cross
the bridge
between the two?
How reconcile
the 'little town'
that cradled
the Word made
flesh
with all this chaos
death and fear?
Bethlehem,
microcosm
of a world gone
mad,
and God
so far away.

Bethlehem,
House of Bread,

birthplace of One
who called himself
the Bread of Life.
Bread for the world,
broken for us,
and all the
Bethlehems
that ever were
or are.
He himself
becomes the bridge,
and once again I
see,
but now with adult
eyes
eternity bursting
into time,
heaven rejoicing,
and God
so very near.

What do you want for Christmas?

At Christmas time we can sometimes be overwhelmed, if we pause from our hectic rushing around, by so much anguish, evil and suffering in our world. We desperately want, although perhaps not desperately enough, hope and joy and peace for all places where these are so glaringly absent. We see the obvious and deep needs of so many human beings but can so easily feel helpless because of their magnitude and our limited ability to do anything about them. Perhaps we need a renewed confidence in God in order to break through the barrier of our powerlessness and resulting apathy. This confidence will come from a renewed openness to receiving the special gift of Christmas.

There is a great difference between needs and wants. We want so many things. Buried beneath our wants, often blurred by them, lie our needs. The greatest need in every human heart is to know that they are loved, to know that to someone they are important, that to at least one other person in this world it matters, really matters, whether they wake up in the morning or not. Many people, far more than we realise, don't have that. There are others who believe that they don't have it, so their pain can be just as great as those who actually don't have it. There are many who cannot accept the fact that they are loveable. This can be due to all sorts of reasons – both from nurture and nature. No matter how many times they are reassured, the reassurance doesn't move beyond a mental acceptance. It doesn't reach the wounded heart or the twisted gut that is silently crying out in anguish for love and acceptance. Maybe, to a greater or lesser extent, we have all known or know what that is like. Because of this disease, and it is a dis-ease – we are not at ease in our spirits, then our capacity to love others is diminished also. The message that we are somehow unlovable has become so internalised that we do not love ourselves either and therefore cannot conceive how our flickering flame of love could possibly warm anyone else's spirit. What a sorry state is ours! It is one of homelessness, of not feeling that we belong, of a confused identity, of sometimes experiencing extreme loneliness even when we are with those whom we know in our heads really care for us.

About two thousand years ago, God made a decision to put his love into action. In the greatest creative, redemptive act of good will that the world has ever seen or ever will see, he sent his only Son into this world, into space and time, to live our life and to die our death so that we might be brought back from our estrangement with God. It was Love that came down at Christmas in the person of Jesus. It was Love that came into our darkness, into our night, God making our homelessness his home, so that everyone who has ever lived, those alive right now and generations yet unborn might have the opportunity to experience the embrace of God. It wasn't God liking us but, rather, so intensely loving us that he chose to come, to experience the very worst that a lost humanity and the powers of evil could fling at him, and emerge from that darkness and dereliction with a new message of hope and joy and peace and love that nothing, not death nor all the forces of hell can rob us of. It is as we choose to abandon or yield ourselves more and more to this love and to turn away from the old imprisoning thoughts, fears, ways of reacting and negative behaviour that we then begin to see God differently, to see ourselves differently and to see others differently.

Christmas is all about giving. Is it? To my mind it is also all about receiving. And maybe we can't be a real giver until we know how to receive.

What do you want for Christmas?

Lord,
the list is endless;
so many things
I wish for,
so much
my heart cries out for.

Here is my list, Lord.
First is hope.
I want hope
to be reborn
in so many weary souls,
in a community
sunk in apathy.
I want hope
in the holding centres
of Zimbabwe,
in the terrorised refugee
camps
of Darfur,
on the winter slopes
of the shattered mountains
of Pakistan,
on the fear-stalked streets
of Baghdad,
in the forgotten famine
of Niger.
In all places
of despair
I want hope.

Next on my list
is joy.
It's a scarce commodity,
Lord,
but I want it
to bubble up
from way beneath the depths
of the anguish,
pain and grief
that shape the stories
of so many lives.
I want joy
for children
who never have had cause
to celebrate,
and joy for those
grown old
and lonely.
In all places
of sadness, grief and
mourning
I want joy.

And then there's peace,
the most sought-after
and perhaps the most elusive
gift of all,
peace that is the healing
balm
for broken hearts

and troubled minds,
peace for countries torn
apart
by civil strife,
peace between nations,
a decommissioning
of minds and hearts,
so bridges may be built
and new communities
based on trust, respect and
friendship
may herald the dawn
of a new day for our world.
In all places of discord,
I want peace.

You ask me what I want
for Christmas, Lord.
I want hope and joy and
peace,
but most of all
it's love I want,
love for myself, for others
and for you.

Without it, all the other gifts
are rendered impotent.
I pause in my requests
and in the stillness hear a
voice,
'Why do you ask
for what already has been
given?
For Love was born at
Christmas,
and is forever present in my
world,
but you must first receive it
before you pass it on.
It is a gift that grows by
sharing.'

At last I understand.
I no longer have a list,
just one request.
All I want for Christmas,
Lord,
is you.

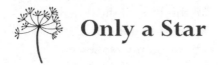

Only a Star

I wonder how long they had been studying the stars, those wise men of long ago? I wonder how many calculations they had made, how many painstaking hours, days, weeks, months, years they had worked and watched and waited? I wonder did they ever think that the years were slipping past and, if something didn't happen soon, then they would be too old to travel? I wonder was it hard to keep hope alive, the hope that someday, in their lifetime, a certain constellation would take place that would be the sign they were waiting for? I wonder did the people around them regard them as crazy, harmless but crazy, to be humoured but not to be taken seriously? I wonder did they ever dare to believe that they were people of destiny? All we can assume is that they were alert for any change in the map of the sky that had become as familiar to them as the palms of their own hands. When the time came, they recognised it, the moment was seized and they set out. One interpretation of the biblical story leads us to believe that their journey was a long one and that they travelled with only a star to guide them for nearly two years. Sometimes when we watch and wait for something for a very long time we don't recognise it when it comes. I wonder how those wise men felt when they noticed something different? Maybe they were imagining it? Maybe it was just an optical illusion? They had made calculation after calculation. But they would have had to come to the point when they had to say, 'Right! This is it! It might not be what we're looking for but it's the clearest signal yet and we've got to go for it!' What a hair-brained journey to set out on – following a star to God knows where!

But it was their time and the time was now. They had the faith to believe that something momentous was going to happen, that their little story was caught up in the larger story of God and that somehow without them that story would be incomplete. Sensing a moment of destiny, grasped by purpose and vision, they set out not knowing where they were going, encountering danger and deception along the way, the political intrigues of Herod and so much else, but all the time focusing their eyes on the star. Their pilgrimage led them to an epiphany moment, a revelation that would change their lives and the life of the world forever.

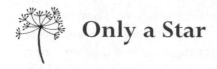 # Only a Star

Only a star to guide them,
three strangers without a name,
yet they willingly went on pilgrimage
when each of them saw the same
constellation ablaze in the heavens,
and this one that seemed like a flame,
travelling through darkness, intrigue and deception
until to the stable they came.

Only a star to guide them
in the darkness of their day
to a place and a meeting so contrary
to what they believed was God's way.
Yet, entering into that stable,
they found they had nothing to say,
and all they could do was to worship
the Child who in front of them lay.

Only a star to guide them
to the place where their searching would end,
to the Light that no darkness can master,
to the One who had come to befriend
a world that was wounded and broken,
that rebelled and would never attend
to a God whose own heart was aching
for them – that their sorrows might end.

Only a star to guide us
in a world paralysed by the pain
of terror and hunger and madness,
of disease and the spirit of Cain;
a world where the powerful triumph
and the poor and the weak cry in vain,
and God's voice goes unheard and unheeded,
and we long for his coming again.

Only a star to guide us
in a land that still doesn't hear
the message that came in that stable
from the One who can deal with our fear
of the other, the stranger, the different,
and he did it by coming so near
that he took on our form and our likeness
to show us that each one is dear.

This year as we journey towards Christmas,
we pray that nothing may mar
our willingness, too, to be pilgrims,
like those strangers who travelled from far.
If, after darkness, intrigue and deception,
we find the door of the stable ajar,
may we enter and fall down and worship,
though to guide us – there's only a star.

What is Truth?

Almost two thousand years ago an event of rare significance took place. We are not told that there were witnesses to this encounter, although there must have been for it is recorded for us in John's Gospel, an encounter far more dramatic than any reality television, however powerful. On one level it could be described as a meeting between the victim and the perpetrator on some sort of truth and reconciliation commission: Jesus representing a Kingdom whose values were not of this world; and Pilate representing the worldly forces of power, greed, manipulation and control. But there the similarity ends, for it is not the 'victim' searching for truth but the perpetrator. There is a fascinating dialogue between Jesus and Pilate. It is like an eternity moment caught in the midst of time. The present is horrendous. Jesus has been through the nightmare of Gethsemane. He has been arrested, deserted by his close companions, brought before Annas and then to trial before Caiphas the High Priest. Already his fate has been sealed by the religious leaders. And now he stands before the secular might of Rome. In a few hours he will be dead.

It is strange, but their meeting, which takes place in the midst of so much violence, has a certain stillness about it, as if this encounter had been destined to take place throughout all eternity, and this was the moment. It is as if the shouts and accusations and clamour fade into the background as these two men face each other. Even as we read it, centuries later, it causes us almost to hold our breath. We know we are on holy ground and there is a moment when we sense, deep in our spirits, that this conversation could have had a different ending. Was Pilate trying to engage Jesus in a philosophical discussion at such a time? Or did the presence of this man, so removed and detached on one level, so present and intimate on the other, unnerve him? Did he catch even a tiny glimpse of something more in this encounter? Did the words of Jesus reach deep into the soul of this tired, cynical, campaign-hardened Roman Consul and for a brief moment tap into the hunger and searching in him, so much so that the question is given voice through the paradoxically unwilling yet eager lips of this man who holds Jesus' life in his hands? 'What is truth?' asks Pilate and, in his resulting confusion, makes a half-hearted attempt to save Jesus from the fate that is surely awaiting him.

His question rings down through the ages. People have used it to genuinely search for a deeper meaning to life. They have sought it on an intellectual level, on a scientific level, on a philosophical level, on a theological level and on a fact-finding level in order to make sense of some of the mysteries and traumas that have deeply affected their lives. What is truth? When we view it as something abstract it becomes doctrine, dogma, ideology, things about which human beings can become passionate, at times even fanatical, so much so that they are willing to torture, maim, kill or be killed in the name of their particular 'truth'. Right throughout history this has been the case. We in Ireland have been no exception to the rule. What actually happens is that a particular ideology or doctrine may contain certain aspects of truth, but when it is raised up as the truth itself, then truth becomes distorted. No human being and no institution can be sole possessor of the truth because in the end truth cannot be contained in doctrine, dogma or ideology. In the end it is mystery because it is embodied in the person of Jesus. Shortly before his death he had declared to his friends, 'I am the way, the truth and the life'. That is what Pilate must have been very fleetingly aware of when he asked that question long ago. Somewhere, however dimly, he must have recognised that he was facing the truth in the person of the man who stood in front of him. The tables were turned on him. It wasn't Pilate who was in control of the encounter. It was Jesus, a King from another Kingdom who had come into the world with a specific purpose, namely to bring truth to the world.

Pilate was a weak, fearful, broken man, but he didn't know it. Perhaps a little glimmer of that truth was getting through to him in that divine appointment long ago. Pilate was also loved and special, but he didn't know it. Perhaps he was hearing a faint whisper of that truth when he was caught in that eternity moment with Jesus. Facing Jesus who is the truth, he could not face the truth and so he asks the question, 'What is truth?' He deflects attention away from himself, the moment passes, a moment in which all heaven held its breath, and Pilate is once again in control of the situation, or so he thinks. If only he had known!

As we face the truth, as we face Jesus, we too are caught in an eternity moment and all heaven holds its breath, waiting for our response. It is not too much to say that the future of the church, of Ireland and of this world depends upon that response!

What is Truth?

What is truth?
One man
representing
the greatest
earthly power
of the time
stands before
another man
and asks
the question.

A question
that rings
down through
the centuries
and is repeated
in every age,
as humankind
struggles
to make sense
of all that
has been done
in the name
of truth.

The other man,
seemingly
defenceless,
vulnerable,
violated,
alone,

his life hanging
by a thread,
a man
who represents
the greatest
power and authority
the world
has ever seen
or ever will
encounter,
the power that,
in the beginning,
created the world,
and the power
that will determine
when its day
is over;
this man stands
before the other,
tortured and broken,
saying little,
but, in himself,
bearing all the
pain and anguish
that has ever been
delivered
by distorted truth.

And, somehow,
the first man

knows
that he is in
the presence
of Truth itself;
Pilate,
caught between
two worlds,
lacking the courage
to opt for Truth.
He washes
his hands
and Truth
is crucified.

Today
we struggle still
with the what
and where
of truth.
So many voices
striving to convince us,
so much confusion,
fear and darkness,
war and mayhem,
threats of mass destruction;
where do we turn
to find an
answer
to our tortured
questioning?

For those with
eyes to see
and ears to hear
and hearts

to understand,
the answer
is the same.
Like Pilate
long ago
we are confronted
with the Truth,
not in theory
or rhetoric
or dogma,
but in the person
of a man,
the other man
whose name is
Jesus.

His way
the way of peace,
of dying to
earthly power,
greed
and pride,
of risking enough
to travel through
the darkness
to the light
of resurrection,
where we know
that we can
stand with him
against a world
that, even yet,
chooses to
wash its hands.

Ecce Homo

Perhaps there has never been a starker choice placed before people than the one that was presented on that day long ago when two prisoners were led out to stand before them and the Roman Governor asked the question, 'Which one do you want me to set free for you?' Two men stood there, two men who had grown up in the same small country, two men who had faced the same national difficulties and struggle, two men who had inherited a history of conflict, hardship, poverty and oppression, two men who lived in an environment of violence, bigotry and hatred, but also an environment that was extremely religious and legalistic. And both of them had the same first name, Jesus, meaning 'the one who saves'.

There was Jesus Barabbas, a leader among his fellows, a freedom fighter, a member of a terrorist organisation known as the Zealots, someone who felt because of the wrongs and oppression of generations that the only answer was the way of violence, to hate, to oppose, to kill. And then there was Jesus the Messiah, also a leader, a man who had experienced the same wrongs, injustices, hurts; citizen of the same country that had been torn apart over the centuries but who chose a different way of liberation and invited others to accompany him – the way of forgiveness, of love, of peace. Both had faith, but for one it was religion, something to which he adhered and which fed his political aspirations. For the other it was a living faith to which everything else was subject. Both were prisoners. One was sentenced to death for inciting people to violence, murder and uprising; the other was sentenced to death seemingly because he urged people to love and to an inner freedom where they knew they were accepted, healed, restored, forgiven, where they had dignity and worth. Both threatened the establishment, but the way of Jesus the Messiah more than that of Jesus Barabbas. One was held in bondage to his past and all that that meant. The other was taking what was good from the past, giving it a new meaning and pointing to hope for the future. You would have thought that, when faced with such a choice, the crowd would obviously have chosen Jesus the Messiah. If we had been there, we would have done that, wouldn't we? Would we?

But the world of Barabbas was the world they knew, the world of smaller, meaner things; things like grievance, resentment, bigotry, bitterness, holding on for grim death to what they had got, not to yield an inch in attitude or patterns of thinking in which they had been conditioned for centuries. It was easier to opt for that. Also, they were afraid: afraid of standing up and being different, afraid of the authorities who were engineering Jesus' death. If you were seen to choose him, stand with him, you could end up being isolated, rejected, even crucified like him! Those who did try to shout for Jesus were drowned out by the others. And many of those who had shouted 'Hosanna!' a few days before when it was the popular thing to do were now adding their voices to those who clamoured for his death.

Jesus still comes. He stands before us and in his very coming offers us the choice. *Ecce homo!* Here is the man! If we dare to choose him it will not be an easy way. It will be a cross-bearing way as it has been for many throughout the years, those who have borne the cross of beginning to see things differently and then being courageous enough to act upon it. It is a hard choice, but one that will mean new life for us as individuals, for this island and for this world. We have to choose – Jesus Barabbas or Jesus the Christ. If we dither, the spirit of Barabbas wins the day.

Ecce Homo

Here is the man
scourged and beaten,
mocked, derided,
purple robe
and crown of thorns.
Alone he stands
before the judgement seat
and waits,
the verdict written
on the aching
heart of God
before the world
began.
No advocate
to plead his cause,
no word of comfort
or of hope.
Only the raucous cries
of those who,
hungering for blood,
cry, 'Crucify!
Crucify this man!'

Here is the man,
the One whose hands
stretched out to heal,
to touch, to bless,
the One who calmed
the storms of nature
and of troubled minds;

whose words reached
deep into their
fearful, tortured hearts
and brought new life
and hope.
Here is the man
who broke the bread
for multitudes,
and to one single,
human soul
spoke words of pardon,
'Neither do I condemn you.
Go in peace!'

Here is the man,
condemned and sentenced
by fanatical religion
and by secular power,
self-centred and
self-seeking,
that down through
centuries
still drag
a God of love,
of mercy and of peace
before the judgement seat
of a world
gone crazy,
hungering for blood.
Yet still he stands

and waits
as the world
he loves and died
to save
still crucifies itself,
still cannot see
or understand
how hatred
can be turned to love,
despair to hope
and war to peace.

Is there then
for us
no hope,
no remedy
for fear,
no advocate
to plead
our cause,
no word of
comfort,
no guarantee
of safety
as frantically
we seek to guess
where terror next
will strike?

Jesus, Lamb of God
Conqueror of death,
Vanquisher of evil,
You take away
the sins of
the world.
Have mercy on us.

Jesus, Lamb of God,
wounded healer,
arms still outstretched
in blessing.
You take away
the sins of
the world.
Have mercy on us.

Jesus, Lamb of God,
majestic in love,
glorious in resurrection,
you take away
the sins of
the world.
Grant us peace.

Here is the man!

Jesus, Remember Me

Within the Christian tradition whenever we think of Holy Week, one of the things we 'remember' is that on that particular day, that first Good Friday, in that place outside the walls of Jerusalem where criminals were put to death there were three crosses. We focus naturally on the middle cross wherein lay and lies our hope of salvation. But on either side there hung a criminal, two thieves that we label now as 'good' and 'bad'. Actually they were both 'bad'. Whatever their past had been in terms of petty crime or a more violent lifestyle, they were now paying the price of a ghastly death. But the one on the middle cross was different. Even they, in their agony, could see that. What had led him to this point, to this terrible fate? The reactions of the two were totally contradictory. One, out of his own pain, resentment, guilt and murky past could not, even at this stage so close to death, face himself. So he projects his guilt and anger outwards to the man on the central cross. 'So you're the Messiah, are you? Prove it by saving yourself – and us, too, while you're at it!' We almost forget about him. He disappears into the shadows of history, only recollected in order to point up the contrast with the other. But the other one fascinates us. We warm to him. He gives us hope. He says what we want to say or would have wanted to say had we been there. We persist in remembering him as the 'good thief'. Out of all the different happenings around that central cross on that unforgettable day, there were two very intimate encounters, eternity moments. One was between Jesus and his mother. The other was between Jesus and this dying thief.

We are told that often the last sense to go when people are dying is their hearing. Even if they cannot respond, it is as if this sense becomes sharpened or heightened. Perhaps drifting in and out of consciousness, overcome by tidal waves of agony, as were the other two, this man would have become acutely aware of the man on the cross next to him. Amid all the other shouts and taunts and noise from the soldier executioners and the spectators what he may have heard was this man's silence, a silence so deep and so profound that it spoke volumes. Something in his silence, in his presence, in the spirit that emanated from the poor mangled body that hung beside him began to have an effect on this thief who had just a few hours left to live. And then his neighbour broke his silence, not with curses or cries of agony as one might have expected, but with a prayer so generous, so extraordinary that it seemed, in one crazy moment, as if the tables were turned, and it was all the rest who were condemned and this one who was free! The dying thief, with his sharpened senses, heard every word. The man said: 'Father, forgive these people, because they don't know what they are doing.' The mockery and the scoffing continued, in fact increased in intensity. Even the other thief joined in, railing against the man beside him. At this point the good thief could bear it no longer and with supreme effort, gasping for breath, he said: 'Don't you fear God even when you are dying? We deserve to die for our evil deeds, but this man hasn't done anything wrong.' And then it was as if there were just two people in all the universe – Jesus and this other. Although nailed to a cross, he turned his whole inner being towards his neighbour and said: 'Jesus, remember me when you come into your Kingdom.' He didn't really know what he was asking for, only that he had encountered someone and something so real yet so mysterious that he didn't want to lose it, whatever it was. Maybe, as someone has suggested, he simply wanted a little corner in Jesus' memory. Certainly he was not prepared for the response: 'I assure you, today you will be with me in paradise.' In the midst of all that he was going through himself, Jesus really heard this man. In his humanity, at this point of total agony and dereliction, God hanging on a cross receives comfort from this very unlikely source, a dying thief who 'stands' with him and, in a strange sense, affirms him by recognising who he is. His cry for mercy is couched in the words, 'Remember me!' It is the last plea or prayer from a dying man. Perhaps when he reached heaven it was also in the form of a question asked with bated breath, hoping against hope: 'Remember me? I'm the one who died beside you. You promised me something then. Do you remember, Lord?'

We come with our cry for mercy for the past, as well as for the present and the future. 'Jesus, remember us. Don't turn us away. Give us a little corner in your memory, an abiding place with you.' We come maybe with the question, 'Remember us? We're the ones who asked you to look out for us when we would come to the gates of paradise. We know we don't deserve it, but because of what you have done for us, we dare to ask.' Every time we come to the sacrament of communion, Jesus himself puts flesh again on the past. He comes to us in the bread and the wine. He really hears us. And in the stillness of the moment he asks the question and responds with the answer at one and the same time, 'Remember me? I am the one who hung on that cross for you. I am the one who hears your cry for mercy. I am the one who loves you. And I have prepared a place for you.'

Jesus, Remember Me

'Jesus, remember me'
is the cry
that comes from many
on their final journey.
It is not death
I fear exactly.
Rather it is the process
of dying.
How will it be for me,
that transition
from one world
to the next?
It is not fear
that taunts me
but rather questions
that sometimes swirl
around
and finish
in the realm
of mystery.

What will that world
be like?
Will I know
the way
to get there?
Will there be
a place prepared
for me?
Or will I have to wander,

searching for some
familiar face,
and for some space
to rest
after the most momentous
journey
I have ever made
since birth?
And if my body
as I have known it
is left behind,
returning to the dust
from whence it came,
what will my new body
look like,
and how will I recognise
those who have gone before?

As the years creep on
sometimes I am cautious
about visiting new places,
of moving house
away from the familiar,
from the security
of what I've always known.
Lord, help me to see
that as I move closer
to that final earthly journey,
I will remember
somewhere beyond memory

the place from which I came,
and to which
I am returning.

Help me to trust
your promise and to look
forward
with expectancy
to what you have prepared,
knowing that you will and do
remember,
and that some day
I, too, will hear
your 'Welcome home'.

It is Accomplished

In Northern Ireland we are tired of hearing the word 'No'. For so long negativity has dominated our thinking and has held back the process towards peace and political stability for which we so desperately long. 'No' can become so overwhelming and so oppressive that people switch off, retreat into apathy or teeter on the verge of a communal depression, so much so that the work of the peacemakers, the reconcilers, has become much more difficult than it was even a few years ago. 'No' becomes almost like another nail in the coffin of dashed hopes, broken dreams and shattered vision.

'No' needn't always be so. There was one 'No' in history that turned the world upside down. It wasn't verbalised but was louder than any cry the world has ever heard. It was a silent scream wrenched from the heart of the God-man who hung on a cross and refused to perform the one miracle the crowd demanded. 'If you are the Son of God, save yourself and come down from the cross!' It would have been so easy and so simple for him to do, but he didn't do it. For three years Jesus had declared through his teaching, his healing, his presence who he was, but by and large people could not see or understand, so would his 'coming down' really have made any difference? It was probably one of Jesus' biggest temptations, but if he had given in to the taunting of the crowd and come down, his action would have entered the world of the nine-day wonder and God's dream for humanity would have been thwarted.

I suppose that the loudest cry wrenched from the heart of all the troubled places in the world, and there are so many, is for peace; peace that is more than an absence of conflict, but that embraces compassion and truth and right relationships, and is even more than all of them put together; peace that is the shalom of God, total well-being for individuals, communities, nations and, indeed, the whole created order. When I speak of peace in that way, it may sound to you like pie in the sky, the beloved community for which we yearn but will never see this side of death. But if we choose to stand on the side of the prophets and with the crucified peoples of this earth then we must give ourselves to it and we must dare to dream.

Jesus had a dream that made him set his face like flint for Jerusalem, where the cost for him was to take upon himself all the sin, the suffering, the anguish and the evil of the world, and to embrace the cross, for the sake of the dream's realisation – the triumph, the victory of love. 'He is our peace,' cries Paul, 'who has broken down the middle wall of hostility between us.'

Like the crowd long ago around that cross, we are all part of a common humanity, broken and wounded, desperately looking for affirmation, security, love, identity and belonging. We beg for signs, we demand proof and it is never enough to fill the bottomless pit inside us. We are scared to look inwards and so project all negativity outwards, looking for scapegoats. Jesus said once to the religious leaders of his day: 'You ask for signs. No sign will be given to you but the sign of the prophet Jonah.' And what was that sign? It was the sign of a poor man preaching repentance. That 'poor man' holds the key to all our dreams as he held it for those on that first Good Friday. We know that they went home in sorrow. Somehow they knew before that day was over that here was God. And precisely because he was God's Son, he couldn't come down. Thank God he didn't. Thank God that because he stayed there until all was accomplished we can dare to dream, we can bear the cost and can even journey home rejoicing!

It is Accomplished

If you are God's Son
come down from there!
Prove it to us.
Perform for us
another miracle
like we heard you did for
Lazarus,
or for the widow of Nain,
or for the young daughter
of Jairus!
Has your power disappeared?
What? Have you no magic
wand,
no conjuror's trick
to save yourself?
In thirty-three long years
is this all you have
accomplished?

The words swarm round him
like flies that feast
on clotting blood.
The taunts and jeers
reach him
through a maze of pain
but have no power now
to tempt him
for he knows something
that the crowd of scoffers
don't.

He knows that he has passed
beyond
the realm of that temptation.
There is no coming down.
And although he is
tormented
by the thought
that even God
has now deserted him,
his spirit so attuned to move
in harmony
with his Father's will,
will in that utter dereliction
still surrender himself
into the Father's hands,
flinging his affirmation of
faith
against the darkness,
'It is accomplished'.

Finished, accomplished.
The task the Father
set before him
now complete.
Finished for that baying,
mocking crowd
around that cross of pain
who watch
with avid, morbid
expectation

every drop of blood
and every anguished twist
of broken body
and every moan of agony.
Accomplished for his fearful
friends
who now watch
from a distance
their dreams destroyed,
their hopes as shattered
as that mangled body
of the one who was once
their leader
and their friend.
Accomplished
for all of humankind
who ever lived
and who are yet to be.
Accomplished, finished too
for you, for me.

We know he is God's Son
not because of some
spectacular miracle
at the eleventh hour
but because
at that eleventh hour
he chose not to come down.
And if it was our sin
that nailed him there
then it was his love
that kept him there
until it was accomplished.

Resurrection Morning

Whenever Jesus set out on his mission to announce the Good News, he took with him his twelve disciples, but also others, among whom were some women. They didn't just tag along. He actually took them. It was a conscious decision on his part. The twelve had a very special role, but so, too, did these women. They were companions on the journey and they played a vital, though largely unrecognised part in announcing the Kingdom of God. They were the ones who supported Jesus and the others in so many ways, caring for their material needs so that they could be freed up to focus on their particular calling, but I'm sure they also did a lot of listening, especially at the end of a long, hard day. They were able, as women have been from time immemorial, to be multi-focused, so they were the carers and chief support group for a bunch of single-minded and, at times, exasperating men! They included someone with a very broken past and someone from the highest political and social circles. They had a vital role to play. Jesus knew this and gave them the opportunity to be witnesses to and for him in ways that were different from that of the twelve, but not lesser. This is most clearly evident in the first resurrection appearances and in the subsequent life of the early church. These women weren't camp followers. They were part of a community of women and men who were finding in Jesus the way, the truth and life, life such as they had never before known. And this, collectively, as well as individually, was the Good News they had to share.

Jesus had no problem in seeing women as equally beloved children of God alongside their male counterparts. He recognised their gifts and called them forth to be used in conjunction with those of men in contributing to the formation of true Christian community. Entering into relationship with him, they began to discover the importance of celebrating who they were in all their uniqueness, women, created in the image of God and equal, not the same but equal, in the eyes of this God who loved them and took them with him to announce Good News. The full demonstration or showing forth of what the Kingdom of God was all about could not be done solely by men or solely by women. It needed both and still does. The God who created humankind in his own image, that image being both male and female, knew this better than anyone and has so created us that we have this natural, inherent, sacred bonding and link with each other.

But apart from a relatively few notable exceptions, the history of the Christian Church does not specialise in singling out women for honourable mention. We are largely classed, if noted at all, among the 'many others' who supported Jesus and his disciples, those disciples having been automatically assumed to be men. By and large it is men who have held the power and the control. Sometimes, under the guidance of the Holy Spirit they have led the Church with a glorious humility and have announced the Good News with boldness and compassion. At other times, perhaps forging ahead without that guidance, they have led us into areas of confusion, condemnation, conflict, hopelessness and even of nightmare. Women disciples by far outnumber the men in the Western world today, yet, in terms of being given official 'permission' to proclaim the Gospel, their number is infinitesimal. In all sorts of informal ways, however, they still find hundreds of opportunities to be image bearers of the Kingdom that are often more powerful and more far reaching than the most eloquent sermon.

How do we find the balance? How do we move from a sense of competitiveness, defensiveness, stubbornness or hurt to that sense of being companions on the journey, walking the road that Jesus has already marked out for us. It is his desire that we should walk it together, not the same but equal in his sight. A ministry composed entirely of men is somehow lopsided and lacking, but equally so would be a ministry composed entirely of women. It seems to me that part of the key lies in recognising our own weaknesses and vulnerabilities, be we men or women. Each one of those first twelve disciples had areas within them that needed to be touched, healed or nurtured by Jesus every bit as much as the inner beings of Mary Magdalene, Joanna, Susanna and all the others. It is out of a recognition of our own fragilities more than boasting of our strengths that true community is born and where Jesus is free to be most powerfully present. And only where Jesus is present can the Kingdom be fully announced by women and men whose lives proclaim resurrection.

Resurrection Morning

It was early, O so early
in the morning when she came.
The night of anguish seemed unending,
who to talk to, who to blame?
All her hopes and dreams were shattered.
Endlessly her tears did flow
for the one who now lay buried
in that garden long ago.

But, drawing near the tomb, she noticed
that the stone was rolled away,
and by the entrance stood two strangers
dazzling in their bright array.
'Why these tears?' their only question,
as she stood there lost, alone,
for all that she could see were grave clothes.
The body of her Lord was gone.

Blinded, stricken by her grieving,
helplessly she turned to go.
But another blocked her pathway,
someone whom she did not know.
Thinking him to be the gardener,
maybe he could give her aid?
Tell her something of what happened,
where the body had been laid?

A moment's silence hung between them,
and all creation held its breath.
Earth and heaven lost in wonder,
seeing life emerge from death.
He spoke one word, no more was needed,
for he called her by her name.
Instantly she recognised him.
Life could never be the same.

For Mary on that Easter morning,
and womankind for evermore,
equality and hope established,
dignity brought to the fore.
Commissioned to be good news bearers,
first the message to proclaim,
'Christ has died and Christ is risen,
Christ will surely come again.'

This the glad good news we carry
to a world in anguish still.
Disbelieving, doubting, fighting,
breeding ground for every ill.
Few there are who heed the message
of a different way to be,
one marked out by truth and justice, grace
abundant, priceless, free.

Could it be that, in that garden,
on that morning long ago
God especially chose a woman
so that she might rise and go
to her brothers, hurt and grieving
with her passion and her grace
to hear from her the glorious message,
'I have seen him, face to face!'

Jesus, risen, now ascended,
reigning by your Father's side,
look upon us, in your mercy.
Heal in us what would divide.
Give your Church, both men and women,
such a vision of your grace,
that together we might carry
your good news to every place.

Sacramental Brokenness

It is one of the loveliest things in the world to share a meal with a friend, to break bread with each other, to be rooted in that sort of hospitality one with the other, to be at home with each other in an eternity moment, a moment of communion, of intimacy. It is truly holy ground. The invitation from Jesus to share a meal with us, as recorded in the Book of Revelation, is very precious and very special, maybe so special that many feel it is beyond their reach. 'Look! Here I stand at the door and knock. If you hear me calling and open the door, I will come in and we will share a meal as friends.' All of us deep down yearn for that sort of relationship. Whether we fully realise it or not, it is the ache in every human heart. Within every human being is a God-shaped hole that nothing and no one else can fill or satisfy, not even the dearest human communion. For those who are already journeying, who have entered the God-friendship, who have heard his 'Hello' spoken deep into their hearts maybe once or many times, there is always more and always the desire for more – more intimacy, more of him.

The whole concept of welcome, of invitation, of hospitality is at the core of the Gospel, at the heart of the Good News. As we experience in a deeper way God's welcome of us, then we are called to extend a similar hospitality to one another and to ourselves. Again and again in Scripture intimacy with God is depicted by an invitation to a meal. This is most poignantly, movingly and eternally presented by Jesus on the night before he dies and becomes the symbol for that intimacy and communion with him and with one another until he comes again. In this most central act of hospitality, of his welcome of us, how we have limited who should come, how we have wounded his heart and how we need to allow the pain in the heart of God to become our pain until it becomes so unbearable that we have no option but to do something about it. In all humility we need to be open and willing to change so that when the invitation is given we might together, in all our littleness and brokenness, break bread, might together receive into our lives his life with all that that implies of healing, of forgiveness, of empowering, of food for the journey and wine for rejoicing. When this begins to happen, then we can authentically be witnesses to a broken, weary, divided, homeless and homesick world that the God of hospitality is reaching out to us, is beckoning us and is welcoming us also.

Sacramental Brokenness

'Until I come again,'
you said,
'do this.
Perform this deed.
Re-enact this special time.
Break the bread
and share the wine
and know that
as you do
you are bonded close with
me
and I with you
and this is
holy ground.

Until I come again
do this,
not only in memory
of one who lived and died,
but who now lives
forever.
Memory is good,
but not enough,
unless it is a spur
to live today
with deeper faith,
with greater integrity,
with more generosity
and with increasing love.
Do this,

so that you have food
for such a journey,
and wine for such rejoicing
at the times of rest
and of community.
And every time
you do so, know
that this is
holy ground.

Until I come again,
receive into your life
my life,
bread and wine,
body broken,
blood poured out,
death which brings life,
forgiveness and renewing,
so that you might be
a body united
in all your diversity,
a symbol and an icon
of my compassion
and my love
for all the world,
a world that,
though it does not
recognise the fact,
is holy ground.

Until I come again
do this.
This is your way
to unity,
to come together
in your brokenness
and find yourselves
again
united in this
feast of love.
This is your way
together to proclaim
good news
that Christ has died,
Christ is risen,
Christ will come again,
and that your brokenness,
your sin, your grief,
your pain
cannot stop the tidal wave
of love
that flows from heaven
in this one act
and equips you even now
to be my messengers
to an anguished world,
and, because of this,
everywhere you place your
feet
is holy ground.'

Dear Jesus,
when you come again,
and even now

you find
in this one central act
with which you have
commissioned us
that we have broken
even further
what was broken
first for us.
We cannot reach agreement
on all the hows
and whys
of who should share
and who should not.
We have taken
what was in your heart
to be a bridge
and have made it
into a wall
that is unscalable,
and the stones from which
that wall is built
come not from holy ground
but at best are stones
of human wisdom
and understanding,
more often
of unyielding wills,
of unexploded myths,
of hearts closed
to the movement of the
Spirit,
of an unwillingness
or an inability
to see the other's truth,

or that each truth
is simply a tiny part
of one enormous truth
that is embodied
not in doctrine,
creed or dogma,
but in you
and in your body
broken for the world,
crucified and risen,
that we and all the world
might once again
be holy ground.

Until you come again,
as we do this
give us the grace
and the humility
to fully enter
this place

of brokenness,
diversity and pain.
And as we seek
to be present
to each other
and to you
across the gaps
may we find it
even yet to be
a place
of holy ground.

St Peter's – *Resurrexit!*

On the last Sunday of July 2005 I slipped into St Peter's Cathedral for the twelve o'clock mass. I had an irresistible urge to do so. Three days previously, the IRA had made their definitive statement that the armed struggle was over and that, henceforward, they would devote their energies to peaceful means in order to achieve their political aspirations. St Peter's is situated at the bottom of the Falls Road, an area that has experienced some of the darkest times of the 'troubles' in terms of enormous suffering, oppression and aggression from every source. Wounds, visible and invisible, still remain and will take many years to heal. I have to confess that as I sat there on that Sunday, my immediate feelings were not those of joy and gratitude but, rather, of incredible sadness for all the wasted lives, lost opportunities, broken dreams and shattered hopes of the last thirty-six years.

On 6 February 2005, after two years of extensive restoration work, St Peter's Cathedral was reopened in a very colourful and moving celebration. The refurbished and restored building is one that can proudly take its place not only in Belfast but among the beautiful cathedrals of the world. It is becoming, along with its Anglican sister Cathedral of St Anne's, one of the places to visit in Belfast. But hand in hand with the refurbishment and restoration of the Cathedral building there is another work of restoration going on in the people, the living stones. I believe that from the shadows, the pain, the anguish of the last years a light can begin to shine that will be a sign of hope for Belfast and the rest of Ireland.

St Peter's – *Resurrexit!*

Twin spires
rise majestically
in all their
refurbished splendour
towering above
the buildings
old and new
that now form part
of downtown Belfast.
Embattled city
torn apart
by your incestuous
relationships
of love and hate,
emerging reluctantly,
yet courageously,
to take your place
among your partners
in Europe.

For nearly fifteen decades
these two spires
have been subconsciously,
yet indelibly,
part of the skyline
of this city.
What stories you could tell
were you to speak.
What heartaches,
celebrations,

joys and nightmares
you have witnessed
in all your lonely years
of pointing to the sky,
willing but unable
to reach down
and touch
the gaping wounds
and oozing sores
of injustice,
poverty
and lawlessness
that are the bitter harvest
of division, prejudice
and unexploded myth,
of economic deprivation,
of antiquated systems
of power and control
that failed to see
the dignity and worth
of every citizen.
Divis,
the very name
synonymous
with the long
hard years
of civil strife,
of plot and intrigue,
of deeds executed
that forever

leave a scar
on a community
already embittered
and despairing
of any life
beyond the present.

Is there resurrection
there for you?
You who have borne
the brunt
of all the years
and tears,
the loyal souls,
the faithful hearts,
the courageous spirits,
the hidden saints
that are the heartbeat
of this parish
of Saint Peter's.

The twin spires
announce to the city
that times are changing.
They declare
that here is a cathedral
until recently
not given its rightful place
in a city
that is as much
its home
as that of its sister
of Saint Anne's.
You have your

bishop's chair,
your cathedral choir,
your blue-robed choir boys,
your unending vigil
of prayer,
your priests
and faithful people.
But more than that,
you bear the name
of one who,
more than any
of the first apostles,
knew the full impact
of what it meant to be
restored
and resurrected.
Emerging from denial,
from brokenness and tears,
from his journey
through darkness
to resurrection life
to truly become
the rock
on which
the Church of Jesus Christ
is built.

You too
have had
your *via dolorosa*,
but now
it's resurrection time
for you
as once again

your doors are opened
to the faithful.
May they embrace
those of every
colour, race
and creed
who in their hearts believe,
and with their voice proclaim
that Jesus Christ
is Lord.
May you forever be
a symbol of unity
and may your twin spires
come to represent
two peoples
different, but united
in declaring
a common humanity,
a common Lord
and their sisterhood
and brotherhood
in him.

 **Disappeared**

All over the world there are people waiting, waiting for news of loved ones who in all probability are dead, but there has been no confirmation, no identification process, no death certificate. Perhaps there is no greater agony than the agony of half-hope, of not knowing. It keeps the mind captive to a frantic questioning, the heart lurching between an infrequent and precarious elation at the slightest snippet of information and an almost total and increasingly familiar despair and brokenness, and the gut twisting with emotion so powerful and deep that it cannot be expressed. In very recent times we have been made much more aware of such nightmare scenarios because of tragedies such as the tsunami disaster in South East Asia and the terrorist bombings that can happen at any time in any place. All of these cause great trauma, but also an ongoing anguish as people wait for the long process of identification to be completed. In spite of all our highly developed technology, there are some whose bodies are never found, some also who are never named and claimed.

But this is no new phenomenon. Throughout the centuries, in innumerable conflicts, perhaps the worst news those 'at home' could receive was the stark message, 'Missing. Presumed dead'. This is hard enough to bear when the conflict is an international one, but it is much more disturbing and sinister when it happens within the borders of the one country, when people who inhabit the same bit of earth, fellow countrymen and women, turn on each other and submit to the process of dehumanisation that can rapidly turn to demonisation where all actions become legitimate. In the latter half of the twentieth century we began to become familiar with the term 'disappeared', largely through the courageous stand of mothers in Argentina. In Buenos Aires a square in the city has been renamed Plaza de los Madres, after the women who silently protested, and still do, about the disappearance of their sons and daughters under a particularly brutal, dictatorial regime. Argentina's disappeared eventually made news; so too did those of Chile, Vietnam, Rwanda, Bosnia and countless other places, many of which we have simply forgotten, like El Salvador or the lost ones from the Biafaran war in Nigeria.

As I write, it is still happening – in Iraq, Afghanistan, Sudan, Zimbabwe and places too numerous to mention. There is a largely silent scream rising up from around the earth that, if it were given voice, would starkly be, 'Where are they?' In the 1970s and 1980s, at the height of Northern Ireland's 'Troubles', a number of people disappeared without trace. They were presumed to have been murdered by the IRA, most accused of being informers. Their bodies were not recovered. They became known as 'The Disappeared'. For years, during this dark period of Irish history, their names were 'forgotten' by all except their loved ones. The whereabouts of their remains lay shrouded in mystery and, for the most part, still do. There is still so much pain, so many unresolved questions. And how much more searing the agony when there are people still alive who have the correct information that would lead to discovery, to the comfort, however stark, of putting to rest not only the remains of these dear ones, but also the torture of wondering that has plagued these survivors night and day over the long years. For the family members of 'The Disappeared' are survivors rather than victims, people of quiet courage and dignity. Several bodies, in the last few years, have been recovered, bringing some measure of peace to broken, weary hearts. But for those who are still waiting, as well as for those who empathise with them, it is their prayer that someone, even yet, might have the courage and the compassion to speak the truth, to give the necessary details that would bring a measure of freedom and healing and peace. In the first decade of this new millennium, when we hope and pray and work for a new Ireland that will fulfil her destiny, a destiny that centres around the call to reconciliation and an acceptance that creates room enough for all, it is not too late to redeem something from the darkness of the past and to contribute to a future, marked by justice, peace, truth – and mercy.

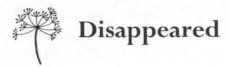

Disappeared

What does it mean
to disappear?
Is it a non appearance,
an absence of presence?
And could that absence
even blur my memory
so that I forget,
whilst constantly striving
to remember
what he looked like,
though I've gazed upon his
face a thousand times
before he disappeared?

There is something instant
about disappearance.
Now you see him,
now you don't.
It is the dark side of magic
with no conjuring trick
to bring the object of
endearment,
the focus of love
back into living reality,
back into the present,
the present that he filled
so powerfully with his life
a thousand times
before he disappeared.
Disappearance means

not to see his face,
to hear his voice,
to rub up against
the habits and the attitudes
that frustrate
and yet endear.
Disappearance leads to
anguish,
to the agony of half hope,
to the torment of not
knowing.
Disappearance trails behind it
the baggage of thousands
of unanswered questions
and nightmarish taunts.
Where is he?
Is he really dead?
Or could it be
a cruel joke,
and one night
he'll lift the latch
and walk through the door
like he's done
a thousand times before
back in those days
before he disappeared.

And if he did not only
disappear,

but was taken,
held and killed,
how did he die?
Was he cold
and frightened
and alone?
Did he call out
for me,
for the comfort and the
ordinariness
of my nearness
like he did in childhood
a thousand times
before he disappeared?

Disappeared.
A single word
that carries with it
a finality and a loss
so great
that all of life
from that point on
is moulded by
this bottomless well
of sorrow and
of wondering.
A double sentence.
For him the death
that came
in darkness and in secret,
quick or long and drawn out
I do not know.
For me a life imprisonment
of never knowing

in what plot of earth
or bog or stone
they covered the remains
of that one life
that touched,
embraced and loved
not only me,
but countless others
in a thousand ways
before he disappeared.

Not for us
the stark comfort
of standing
in the company of the
faithful,
to watch his body
committed to the ground,
or hear the words,
'earth to earth,
ashes to ashes,
dust to dust,
in sure and certain hope
of resurrection.'
No word
down through the years,
no voice of hope.
Simply the statement
echoing endlessly
through our tortured nights
and anguished days,
heavy with the notes of
doom,
'Disappeared!'

A Mother Speaks

(In memory of Jean McConville)

Born – 7 May 1934. Taken from us – 7 December 1972. Recovered – 27 August 2003. Laid to rest – 1 November 2003. Those words, along with the only surviving photograph her children have of her, form the front cover of the service booklet for the funeral mass of Jean McConville. Jean disappeared from Divis Flats in West Belfast in 1972. A Protestant by birth, aged thirty-seven, married to a Catholic, a widow and mother of ten, she was abducted from her home by eight men and four women, all masked. The IRA allege that she was an informer, a claim vigorously denied by her family, who believe that she was abducted because she gave assistance to a dying soldier shot outside her flat. They always hoped that her body would be found, that they could give their mother a Christian burial and that they could begin to move on in their lives. Not only did they have to suffer the immediate trauma of the night of her abduction, but the subsequent weeks of trying to survive without her, and then being split up as a family, the authorities sending them to different institutions.

On the first day of November 2003 I stood with about two hundred other mourners in a Lisburn cemetery, as the remains of Jean McConville, missing for thirty-one years, were finally laid to rest. For two years we had been praying that if no one was going to come forward with accurate information regarding the whereabouts of the Disappeared, then the earth itself would yield up its dead. On the 27 August 2003 that was exactly what happened and, two months later, after all the tests and identification processes had been carried out, her children were able to begin the journey of closure on a nightmare that had lasted for most of their lives. The coffin was already in the ground when someone stepped forward with a little statement about peace that they asked the priest to read, and then one of the grandchildren released a white dove. The dove flew up, paused, hovering above us, and then encircled the cemetery twice, as if bestowing a benediction upon the mourners, after which it disappeared into the heavens. A gasp went up from the crowd. Some wept. I was conscious only that it was All Saints' Day and that, in some mysterious way, we were being reassured that Jean's spirit was finally and fully released to God, and that her children might at last begin to move on from a past that had so horrendously imprisoned them. This is their time and it is the right time. They have a song to sing from their broken place that the world needs to hear. I believe that their story, their witness can contribute to the creation of a new and just society and even to the emergence of the beloved community for which we yearn.

A Mother Speaks

(In memory of Jean McConville)

It was Advent when I left
you,
a time of hope and promise,
but for you a desolation,
an endless questioning,
a deep rejection and betrayal,
abandonment and loss,
unending nightmare and
bewilderment.
How many times I've heard
you
calling in the night
'Mother!'
and I, powerless to reach
you,
my agony matching yours.
No reassuring word of
comfort
to touch you in the
blackness.
Only the stark response
echoing in the emptiness,
one word,
'Disappeared!'

It was Advent when they
took me
into the night where no star
blazed,
into the darkness of trial

and lonely execution.
No voice raised in protest,
no recognition of
vulnerability,
no plea for mercy
that you, my ten beloved,
might have your mother back
to cherish you and nurture,
to do the best I could
for you.

For over thirty years
no Advent dawned again for
you.
Only the cycle of recurring
fear,
of not knowing
where I was,
or who you were.
Identity disintegrated,
frantically searching for
belonging
and never really knowing
a place within yourselves
that resonated with a sense
of peace and hope.

And then – it happened!
The remains of this body
that carried you in love

and gave you birth
were given back.
Past, present and future,
Advent has returned for you.
While not fully redeemed,
the past is now restored.
The present brings an end
to feverish searching.
You've laid my body
in the hallowed ground
and prayed for me.
You've finished something
so that, even yet, my
children,
you may begin again.
The future now is yours – for
claiming.

From that Advent place
beyond the grave, I speak.
Know that, as on All Saints'
Day,
the dove circled
and soared above you,
my spirit, too, has taken
wings.
I stand innocent
of all accusations
before my Maker and my
Lord.
I am whole now and
complete,

and in eternity, I am near to
you,
so near.

I watch for you,
and in the communion of
saints,
I pray for you
that you become
all that is in my heart
and in the heart of God.
So raise your heads,
walk tall and journey well,
for in the eternity of Advent
I wait for you
with hope – and love.

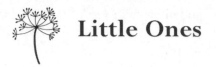 # Little Ones

What joy babies and little children can bring into our lives! I have never had children of my own, but have had the great gift of seven nieces and nephews whom I love dearly. The childlike part of me revelled in their childhood with all its wonder, trust and openness. They gave me permission to be a child again in their company. Now that they are adults, I rejoice in their journeys as I see how the precious individual characteristics have been nurtured and encouraged to shape them into the wonderful, vibrant young women and men they are today. I am now a great aunt! More little people have entered my life bringing renewed awe and joy and fun! Two of them are sisters and entered this world within the last few years, the first being born in Holy Week 2003 and the second in 2005. In the first week of each of their lives, before I had any opportunity to discover some of the unique traits in their personalities, I wrote the following reflections for them and have subsequently been amazed at the accuracy of what seemed to be revealed to me at those times. Like all of today's children, Ruth and Rebecca Mary have entered a tough and rapidly changing world, but they are surrounded by love and nurtured in faith that will give them courage, and hopefully even joy for the journey ahead. For all the little ones whose lives we touch, I offer that same prayer.

Little Ruth

You began
your earthly journey
in the spring;
a time of daffodils
and sunshine,
of birdsong
and blossoming things,
of colour, growth
and newness,
and you
the newest
and the sweetest
gift of all.

You began
your earthly journey
in the spring,
a time of war,
of darkness and confusion,
of faltering peace
agreements,
of fears and agonies,
and oh so fragile
hopes,
and yet
you chose to come,
(or were you sent?)
at Easter,
almost as if
you knew

that this was
Holy Week,
so that the very air
around you
seemed sanctified
and blessed,
as if the angels
sang their songs
for you,
as you began
your earthly journey
in the spring.

What stories you could
share with us
had you the words,
about the world
from which you came
and to which
one day
you will return.

Was it a journey
through a thousand
stars
or a place
so close,
yet so mysterious,
a kingdom
that is all about us,

a world
invisible but real?
Did an angel
lift the latch
for you,
and did you
slip across the threshold
to begin
your earthly journey
in the spring?

For now, you sleep,
guarding those precious
secrets
that so soon
will fade
and be hidden, too,
from you.
But in these special days
you know them still,
you carry with you
the vestiges of heaven,
as you begin
your earthly journey
in the spring.

May the road
you walk
through life
be holy,
blessed
at every turn.
May you dance
and sing

and weep
and laugh,
and sometimes
pause to hear
the voices
that one day
will call you
back across
the threshold
to that world
from which
you came.
May you ever
live your life
on tiptoe,
conscious of
the 'something more',
that ever beckons,
and may it
always give
you courage
to remember
that you began
your earthly journey
in the spring.

Rebecca Mary

You took us by surprise
so quickly did you come,
out of breath,
tumbling into this world
as if you had so much
to catch up on,
to see and to experience
that a lifetime seemed too
short
to do it all.

And now you're here.
The family is complete
and you're content,
as if you knew
there was a place prepared
for you
and you had to come and
claim it.

We wait to know you.
Already we have fallen for
you
as you foreknew we would.
Immediately wrapped
around
a little finger
of infinitesimal size,
we are your willing slaves
ready to hear the faintest

whimper
or to interpret
the first expression of
delight.

They gave you strong names,
proud names of holy
women.
Is there a mystery
in the naming
that will pass on to you
something of the mantle
of Rebecca and of Mary?

Rebecca of the old covenant,
chosen of God,
full of hospitality
of the heart,
willing to become a pilgrim,
to travel to a far country
that a new nation
might be born,
and shaped and moulded
to fulfil their destiny
as the people of God.

Mary of the new covenant,
chosen also of God,
poor and lowly,
yet in herself

being the means through
which
the Word of God
becomes incarnate
in human flesh
her servant 'yes'
the open door
through which
redemptive love
flows forth
for all of humankind.

What are our dreams for
you,
little one with such noble
and awesome names?
May you pick up
the courage, the loyalty
and the spirit of adventure
embodied in the old
and honoured name
Rebecca.

May you have
the openness, the trust,
the rejoicing heart
and quiet devotion
of that first woman
of the new creation,
Mary.

Blessed are you,
Rebecca of the pilgrim heart,
and Mary of creative love.
And when your journey
here is done
may you find
another place prepared for
you
where these two
women of God
reclaim their namesake
and bid you
welcome home.

Fáilte Little One

For centuries in Ireland we have had two cultures, often at loggerheads with each other, each one clearly defined and shaped by its religion, its political allegiance, its traditions, its aspirations, its interpretation of history. On rare and notable occasions throughout the centuries there has been a crossing over on the part of some who, prompted by a particular cause or inspired by some idealism, entered the territory of the 'other' and discovered there the gift of a common humanity. By and large these sorties were short-lived. However, they did bear witness to what could be but has been a long time in coming. The more recent years of civil strife have acted as a stumbling block in this process for some, but as a door of opportunity for others. The much greater freedom of movement between different countries along with the peace process in the North of Ireland has encouraged many to seek to make their home in this island. While we are not yet a rainbow-coloured nation, the entry of our new neighbours is highlighting for us again the importance of hospitality and of welcome and is blurring the edges of our old divisions. For those with eyes to see, we are also being shown the wonderful gift of diversity and what riches we have to share with each other. Some of the very special members of our expanding island family are little ones who have been adopted from other countries. Everyone needs to know that they belong, that to someone they are special. These children didn't choose Ireland; Ireland chose them. May they always find among us a generosity of spirit and a place called home.

Fáilte Little One

Welcome, little one.
The land of one hundred
thousand welcomes
stretches out its arms to you
in love and in acceptance.
You have travelled far
for one so small
to find a place called home.

Is your heart
full of wonderings,
your soul of questionings?
Is there within you
a subliminal tug of war;
on the one hand
a spirit of adventure
that reaches out
to embrace
what this new culture,
strange   land   and   alien
customs
offer you;
on the other
a sense of homesickness,
an unexplored yet potent
yearning to return
to the familiarity
of a land you hardly know
yet from   whose   dust   you
came

and, had life been different,
would have been for you
a place called home?

The eyes of your ancestors
gaze at us
through your child's eyes,
and see a place
so strange and far away
from what they've always
known.
And yet, they urge you on,
these old ones,
no going back,
no giving up,
but rather an acceptance
of the fact
that by your coming
you create a bond
invisible but strong
between that vast
and mighty land
from which you came
and this green island
that is now your home.

In yourself you are
a bridge,
a vital link,
an instrument of peace,

not Chinese or Irish,
but citizen of the world,
part of a common humanity,
beloved and beautiful,
gifting others
in this orphaned world
with faith and hope
that for them also
there can be
a place called home.

For now, we pray
that you may rest secure
safe in the arms of those
to whom you are entrusted
as a gift.
May you ever be for them
a sheer delight and joy,
and may they always be for
you
a place called home.

A Wedding Prayer

The whole concept of marriage has changed greatly over the years. Certainly in the Western world, entering into a special relationship of love and commitment and sealing that commitment with vows taken before God and in the presence of the family of God is no longer the norm. Many seem to prefer trying it out and leaving an easily accessible exit process if it doesn't work. It has to be said that there are others who don't see the point in getting married but who do remain faithfully committed to each other throughout their lives. Those who have a God-dimension to their lives, those who are people of faith know that this special relationship between a woman and a man is somehow sacred. They know that their journey together through life will have many hardships and obstacles as well as joys and blessings. They believe that, however well intentioned, they are not going to make it on their own. Their wedding day, therefore, takes on a much deeper significance. It is a precious time where they are asking God to be the third person in their relationship, to protect, guide and bless them and to draw them ever closer to himself and, as a consequence, to one another. If they are blessed with the gift of children, then they are also seeking that supernatural grace for them.

A Wedding Prayer

May this day be always special
as you recall it through the years.
May its love and gladness brighten
days of shadow and of tears.
May your friendship ever growing
make you good companions through your life
may give and take, the joy of sharing
mark your way as man and wife.

As you travel on this journey
give each other space to grow
so that separately and together
others seeing you may know
what you bring to one another
is the fruit of being true
to the voice of God within you
always faithful, ever new.

May your home be one that welcomes
the lonely soul, the tired guest.
May they find within its sanctuary
grace and goodness, peace and rest.
As you furnish it with laughter
fill its emptiness with love,
may you know the quiet presence
and the wisdom from above.

May your roots in Ireland keep you
always open to the stranger.
May your faith in God protect

you and yours from every danger.
May the ties of family bless you
old and young united be,
and may difference serve only
to produce pure harmony.

May you celebrate your marriage
every day that God allows.
May he bless you in this union
keep you faithful to your vows.
And as we your friends surround you
we wish you this and every day
'Long life and happiness together!
God be with you all the way!'

Difficult Conversations

I work in Restoration Ministries, a non-denominational organisation seeking to promote healing and reconciliation. Although based in Belfast we are open to the whole island of Ireland and beyond. We are very small, but in what we do we attempt to be image bearers of what is possible for those who have a pilgrim heart and a vision of the beloved community for which we long. A major part of our work is simply to listen, to provide a safe place where people can come and tell their story and be heard. The more public side is, through various events, projects and gatherings to give people from all traditions and backgrounds opportunities to build bridges both within themselves and externally with others who are different from them. To put it another way, we seek to put people in touch with one another at a deep and more challenging level than that of a superficial and cautious politeness. One such project has been to run a series of 'Difficult Conversation Evenings'. This was in response to the challenge of how we move beyond the niceness and cosiness of some of our 'safe' encounters to facing the starker questions and the 'nakedness' of some of our differences. People have been encouraged to voice and to understand their own and others' beliefs, values and identities. This in turn has led to a greater mutual respect and an increasing acceptance of diversity as being something positive and enriching.

On one of our earliest conversations which happened to fall during the season of Lent, we asked a Catholic Sister, native of County Mayo, to lead those of us who were not of her tradition through the Stations of the Cross and the reasoning behind them. She was a little apprehensive because of some of the more vocal Protestants within the group. 'What will happen,' she asked me nervously, 'when I come to Veronica wiping the face of Jesus? I know it's not in Scripture, but it is part of tradition.' I replied that part of the purpose of the evening was that we would learn from each other. Veronica passed off without incident! In fact, the whole experience was a very moving one. One man who had been brought up a staunch Presbyterian, native of County Antrim, was particularly touched. A few days later he told me that he had that very afternoon been to one of the local Catholic Churches and had gone around the Stations of the Cross on his own and that he was going to use that particular spiritual exercise as his main devotion for the rest of Lent.

Difficult Conversations

Tentatively
I stretch out a hand
across the divide,
across the chasm
in whose depths
swirl centuries
of misunderstanding,
fear, mistrust
and hatred.
Our fingers touch.
Strange that they should feel
the same as mine.
There is life there
and warmth
and if I dared
to stretch
just a little bit farther
there could be
a handclasp.

I hesitate.
I am afraid.
What if this
is just a trap
to lure me over
to the other side?
That having got
a hold of my hand,
a relentless grip
will pull me,

against my will
and my convictions
over to the strange land
which will be, for me,
the point of no return,
no longer belonging
to one side
or the other,
an obscuring of my identity.
I dare not look
into the other's eyes
for fear
that I might yield,
if I saw there
a hesitant smile
of welcome.
Instead
I look down again
deep into the chasm.
The familiar demons,
like sirens of old
entice me back
to the negative security
of what I've always known.

But wait a bit!
The demon voice inside me
whispers,
'What if my grip is stronger,
and I can pull hard enough

to bring "them" to me,
for, after all,
I and those I represent
possess the truth.
It is they
who are in error,
they who need
to see the light.'

Standing on the brink,
the choice is mine,
to risk a reaching out
to all that is positive,
open and enriching,
or to plunge yet again
into the darkness
of suspicion, exclusion
and division.
From somewhere
I hear a voice,
familiar, yet strange,
old, yet ever new,

'Choose this day
whom you will serve.'
I have a choice
to serve the old demons
of my ancestors
or the God
who entered into
the most difficult
conversation of all
with humankind
by sending Jesus,
the Word made flesh
to become the bridge
that leads us back
to one another
and to him.

Restoration House

For nearly twenty years Restoration Ministries has sought to be a little icon of unity in diversity, of bridge building in a torn and divided community, of hospitality, of healing and of prayer. While the message of restoration is carried out around the island of Ireland and farther afield through our newsletters and through retreats and conferences, it is at our base, Restoration House in Dunmurry, that the coalface work is done. Prayer is at the centre of what we do and it seems, as the years go by, that the bricks and mortar of this old and beloved house are absorbing some of the many prayers offered here every day. We rejoice that people find within these walls a place of safety and beyond that a sense of the presence of God.

Restoration House

May this be a house of welcome,
a place of peace where all can come,
always finding hearts to listen
and an atmosphere of home.

May it be a house for pilgrims
for whom the road has been too long
who need the space to rest awhile
before they journey on.

May it be a house of meeting
that people, seeking, here may find
brave new ways of being open
and uniting heart and mind.

May this house be one of healing
for those lost or in despair
to find fresh courage, peace and hope
and answers to their prayer.

Some call us a house of safety
when they share what they have found.
May we always treat their story
as a place of holy ground.

May peace exude from every room
because these walls are steeped in prayer.
May those who enter sense God's presence
and the love of those who care.
May the name that we were given
be lived out with each new day.
May this house be always ready
for weary souls along the way.

May we celebrate the journey
on the way to being whole
and may our song be always only
'Jesus' – he restores my soul.

 # Sixty

When I was young, or even in my mid-thirties or forties, sixty seemed generations away and, if I thought about it at all, it was of an alien world that had little or no connection with where I was at present! The years have flown by and now I find myself at the beginning of a new decade. Inside I don't feel any different to the far-away girl in her twenties or the hopefully maturing woman in her thirties and forties. It is only the externals that remind me that this is an especially particular milestone. I have received state pension forms. I now get free prescriptions. Other people my age have retired and are pursuing various interests for which they may not have had the time before. But in my inner being, I still have the urge to experience more, more of living, more of God, to keep journeying, which, in my case, means to keep following the vocation of reconciliation. Even if ill health or fragility or old age demand an outer giving up, vocation is something from which there is no retirement!

When I look back I am full of gratitude. What a privileged generation ours was! Those of us who now are in our sixties were young people in the 'sixties'. Maybe I am biased, but there never was a time before or since that was so brimming over with possibilities and hope, especially for those of us in the western world who were blessed with the status of students. There was a new global awareness. Social consciousness was aroused especially by the music of the time, and there was a real conviction that we actually could do something to make this world a better place and a more just and peaceful planet. How quickly the 'sixties' passed, taking with them the hope for a better Ireland, let alone a better world, as we were plunged into a nightmare from which, thirty-seven years later, we are still struggling to fully emerge. Whether we realise it or not, what has happened during that time has served to change and to shape our lives in ways that we could never have imagined, some for better, some for worse. For some of us, the formative years of the 'sixties', with their openness, their freedom and the inspiration of some remarkable people, gave us, in conjunction with our faith, a rock foundation that not only steadied us in hard times, but gave some a vision, an endurance and a conviction to keep on praying, hoping and working for the promised land of peace and reconciliation.

When I look back, I am sometimes overawed at the way God has guided and protected me, most importantly often protected me from myself! There's an old hymn, one line of which says, 'Standing somewhere in the shadows you will find him'. Compared to what is up ahead, I know that I have met him and found him, and he has met me and found me in the shadows. From this vantage point I thank God for those shadows and for the glimpses that keep me going. But the dreams, the faith, the hope I have today are only a shadow of what is up ahead. The best is yet to be. I think that, for me, the dream has always been that of a beloved community, a restoration of right relationships between ourselves and God, with our own inner beings and with one another, not for ourselves alone, but so that we might be a sign of hope for the world.

Because I happen to have been born in this island, then that dream is incarnated in Ireland. But its roots go deeper than that. Its roots, I believe, are in another Kingdom, the Kingdom of Heaven. I have a deep sense that lies within the realm of mystery that the call to the ministry of reconciliation came to me before I was born. I do remember once, when I was in my twenties, standing looking up at the Wicklow Mountains and feeling almost a hand of destiny upon me, and sensing that there was hope for Ireland, a hope that was rooted in God. I have stood in a clochan in the Dingle Peninsula and sung the doxology at the top of my voice and with a full heart, and have heard in the spirit the communion of saints joining in. I have walked the hills and beaches of my beloved Donegal and sensed a deep kinship with Colmcille, the dove of the church and with all the faithful companions on the journey who, throughout the centuries, have loved and believed and dreamed dreams and seen visions, and who have rejoiced, even in the midst of the fiercest trials, never tiring of announcing Good News or of believing that the beloved community was possible. They died in faith, as the writer to the Hebrews said, but still in the shadows, not having received all that God had promised. Perhaps we will too. But the dream is still there, and the faith to keep on working and praying and believing that if, in all its brokenness, Ireland can, in the company of Jesus, fulfil its destiny, a destiny that will be manifested in the restoration of that hospitality that is the core of the Gospel, then we have that good news to announce to the rest of the world.

 # Sixty

They tell me
that sixty is the new forty,
that this could be
the time when life begins.
And suddenly it is here!
The postal delivery
though expected
in some vague future
that will not really
touch my life
contains the forms
that tell me
I am now of age
to claim the pension.
It can't be me!
It is some other person
with a similar name!
Or else the vast bureaucracy
has got it wrong.
Within me there is no sense
of winding down
or slowing up,
only that sense of urgency
that tells me that,
although I've lived
six decades of my life,
still up ahead
there is once more a time
when life begins.
Those of us

who now are sixty
remember the sixties
of our youth,
a time of social
consciousness,
of flower power,
and student barricades,
and music that became
a prophetic voice
telling the world
that times were changing,
and calling us
to search for answers
that were blowing in the
wind.
We were the generation
who walked with JFK
and Martin Luther King,
who went to San Francisco
with flowers in their hair
and who really were
convinced
that we would overcome
some day,
so that for all the world
there could yet be a time
when life begins.

I look back
to days of civil rights,

to times when
all seemed possible
and when it wasn't
there was always green
chartreuse
and 'Sergeant Pepper's
Lonely Hearts' Club Band',
and the one road
and the comfort
of bridges
over troubled waters
and new songs
to be sung.
And with a heart
that overflows
with gratitude,
I remember
the charismatic leaders
of our youth
who pointed us
to vistas of opportunity
where we might yet become
makers of peace,
builders of community,
and bearers of hope
in a world that
so quickly changed
from happy ever aftering
to the crude reality
of civil strife,
of lives destroyed,
of homeland torn apart,
so that it seemed
that never could there

be a time again
when life begins.

To live six decades
of my life.
I take them out
and count them over
one by one
like precious holy beads,
each one a prayer,
some bright with promise
and sparkling with youth,
some radiant with
the happiness of discovery
and fulfilment,
some tarnished with the
humdrum
of existence,
some broken and
irreplaceable
as dear ones have departed
or life has dealt
its cruel blows,
or in deluded fantasy
decisions made
and trust misplaced
caused anguish
fathomless and searing,
and hope seemed crushed
beneath the weight
of all the cares
of years.
Yet always,
like a golden thread

in every age and stage
the deep conviction
this is the time
when life begins.
And so to face the future
in a world
and in a time
more fragile, frightened
and confused
than any that
have gone before.
For that beloved generation
just behind
the age of sixty
confines me to the
annals of history!
Yet, as for me,
so too for them
how fast
the years will run.

As I hand each year
and decade
back to God,
the call is still the same,
to live each day
as if it were the time
when life begins,
with all its promise,
newness, hope
and grace,
knowing that up ahead
the best is yet to be,
and that, one day,
leaving even time
itself behind,
I shall step
across the threshold
to that place
where life begins.

Donegal

Each one of us has a special place in our lives, somewhere that we feel rooted and connected. For me, one such place is Donegal. It has always been part of my life and of the lives of generations before me. It's a threshold place, almost as if at any moment a veil would be lifted and you would find yourself in that unseen world that is all about us, so near and yet so mysterious. Its rugged, wild beauty, its ever changing sea and sky, the familiar security of its embracing mountains, the long stretches of untamed shorelines, the sheep paths that lead one with unshakable confidence to old trysting places that evoke warm memories of long ago, the smell of burning peat lingering on the evening air and always the welcome both from those now present and from the unseen crowd of witnesses – all these and many more are gift and, perhaps, a little glimpse, albeit like a dim image in a mirror, of heaven.

# Donegal

The smell of smouldering
peat
lingering on the evening air,
long shadows cast
by late summer sun,
rose tinted sky
hinting at a bright tomorrow
a lonely seagull's plaintive
mew,
seeking its rocky resting
place,
and that, to me,
is Donegal.

Giant waves
pounding the shore,
glistening spray
flung high into the air
at Breaghy Head,
sand blowing, knife-sharp
along the deserted strand
at Marble Hill,
bent grass tossing like a
green sea,
dancing in time to the
merciless gale,
and that, to me,
is Donegal.

Quiet water
silently filling
the peaceful inlet
of the Back Strand,
separating us
for a tide-time only
from our neighbours at Ards.
Full moon, leaving a pathway
of silver light
shimmering on the midnight
estuary
along which weightless feet
might glide;
across Sheephaven Bay
the lights of Downings
vying with the twinkling
stars,
and that, to me,
is Donegal.

Muckish,
you reign supreme,
ageless mountain,
at one moment
standing starkly clear
in all your purple-blue
beauty
against a cloudless sky,
the next
shrouded in mystery,

as rain and mist
hide you from view,
and we are caught
between the loneliness
of missing you
and the strange comfort
of knowing that,
although we cannot see you,
you are ever near,
and that, to me,
is Donegal.

Light from a window,
smoke rising from the
chimney,
bright faces round the fire
and, in the shadows,
the gentle presence
of those who've passed
beyond,
yet, in that mystery of
communion,
are with us still.
Chairs rocking on the
familiar
unevenness of flagged floor,
good books, like trusted
friends

stacked ready to be read
again,
stories to be told,
familiar stories, handed down
from one generation
to the next,
and songs, the sound of
music,
of singing in the very stones,
that stir the senses,
lift the heart
and bring to life again
those bygone times,
and that, to me,
is Donegal.

It was a special gift
you gave us, God,
that we might be a people
whose roots go deep
into the wild beauty,
the untamed loveliness
of this little bit of earth
that we have come to know
as Donegal.

A Prayer of Thanks

Thank you, God,
for hearts awakening
to a new rhythm,
the drumbeat
of a common humanity.

Thank you for eyes
that see beyond the label
to the person
and recognise that difference
is good.

Thank you for ears
that hear a different
incantation
than the dehumanising
chants and slogans
of opposing camps,
a song of hope and unity.

Thank you for minds
into which the light
that no darkness can master
now shines,
bringing a knowledge
of truth
that is not 'ours' or 'theirs'
but is embodied
in the person
of Jesus.

Thank you for voices
that speak out with courage,
whose tones are those
of generosity
and welcome.

Thank you for feet,
swift-winged and ready
to carry the good news
of peace.

Thank you for hands
no longer raised in clenched
fist,
but open,
reaching out in friendship,
becoming human bridges
for a new tomorrow.

Thank you for difficult
conversations
that lead us to new
understanding,
deeper compassion
and into your upside-down
kingdom
of mercy, justice,
truth and peace.

Thank you, God. Amen.